Rahim Ke 50 Dohe

Rahim Ke 50 Dohe

50 Lessons for Entrepreneurs

Prof (Dr) Sanjeev Chaturvedi

GenNext Publication

ISBN: 978-93-5324-626-6

"An Imprint of Kalpaz Publication"

First Published, 2021

Published by

GenNext Publication
5, Ansari Road
Daryaganj, New Delhi-110002
Phone: 9811692060
E-mail: gennextpublication@hotmail.com

Printed at: Gyan Press, Delhi.

This book is dedicated to
my mother late Shrimati
Sheela Chaturvedi (Ammaji)

Acknowledgement

This book was in my mind for more than a decade now. When I joined as a full time faculty, after very illustratious and remunerating career of corporate world, in 2005 there were two observations I made. One there is lot of Management Books on Chankya (or Kautilya as they call him) and second there were some great research work done on Rahim in various Universities and institutions. But there was not much written on Rahim dohes and its learning for management students and public in general. However, the idea remained at the background and could not work more on the subject. But during 2005-2020 I wrote three more books on management/entrepreneurship.

However, the destiny brought me to Tashkent, Uzbekistan as Advisor-India Uzbekistan Entrepreneurship Development Centre (IUEDC) –a Government of India and Uzbekistan Joint Project. During this time, I have a chance to visit Baburs birthplace which is now called Andhijan. I had a chance to visit Andhijan and also the remains of Baburs Birthpalace. This triggered once again the memories of the book writing on Rahim and I started it once again. I can now see it in a final book shape and feel lucky and enlightened to be a part of Rahim's great history and knowledge.

I would like to thanks all my teachers/professors/friends and family members who supported me in this wonderful journey of academics. I also like to thanks my critics also who gave me the energy and determination, to prove them wrong. This book has not been completed without the support and love of my wife Richa and children Vartika and Vedant. They have brought a lot of stability in my career and zeal to fight against all odds.

I am highly obliged to Kalpaz Publications, who have been supporting me over the years and taking great risk of publishing my book. I really salute to their constant support and encouragement.

Finally, I now offer this book to all readers with great humility and modesty for allowing me to write a book connecting Rahim and Entrepreneurship in this turbulent times of Covid-19. I am confident that my mistakes will be ignored and encouragement will be given for making this attempt.

Rahim's Biography

Abdul Rahim was the son of Bairam Khan, Akbar's trusted guardian and mentor, who was of Turkic ancestry. When Humayun returned to India from his exile, he asked his nobles to forge matrimonial alliances with various zamindars and feudal lords across the nation. Humayun married the elder daughter of Khanzada Jamal Khan of Mewat (present Nuh district of Haryana) and he asked Bairam Khan to marry the younger daughter.

Gazetteer of Ulwur (Alwar) states:

> After Babur's death his successor, Humayun, in 1513 was supplanted as ruler by the Pathan Sher Shah Suri, who, in 1545, was followed by Islam Shah. During the reign of the latter, a battle was fought and lost by the emperor's troops at Firozpur Jhirka, in Mewat. However, Islam Shah did not lose his hold on power. Adil Shah, the third of the Pathan interlopers, who succeeded Islam Shah in 1552, had to contend for the empire with Humayun.[3]

In these struggles for the restoration of Babur's dynasty Khanzadas apparently do not figure at all. Humayun seems to have conciliated them by marrying the elder daughter of Khanzada Jamal Khan, nephew of Babur's opponent, Khanzada Hasan Khan Mewati, and by requiring his minister, Bairam Khan, to marry the younger daughter of the same Mewati.[3]

Abdul Rahim was born in Delhi (Indian NCT)[8] to Bairam Khan and the daughter of Jamal Khan of Mewat of modern-day Haryana. After Bairam Khan was murdered in Patan, Gujarat, his first wife and young Rahim were brought safely from Delhi to Ahmedabad and presented at the royal court of Akbar, who gave him the title of 'Mirza Khan', and subsequently married him to Mah Banu (Moon Lady) sister of Mirza Aziz Kokah, son of Ataga Khan, a noted Mughal noble.[8]

Navratnas of Akbar

Later, Bairam Khan's second wife, Salima Sultan Begum (Rahim's stepmother) married her cousin, Akbar, which made Abdul Rahim Khan-e-Khan also his stepson, and later he became one of his nine prominent ministers, the Navaratnas, or nine gems. Aside from being a poet he was also a general and was sent to deal with the Rajput forces of Maharana Pratap after the latter had managed to restore the territories lost in Haldighati. He was defeated by the Pratap's son, the future Rana Amar Singh in a quick battle after which he retired from military life and dedicated his life to cultural development.

His two sons were killed by Akbar's son Jehangir because they were not in favour of Jehangir's accession to the throne at Akbar's death. He is considered a Persophile.[9]

Major works[edit]

Apart from writing various *dohas*, Rahim translated Babar's memoirs, *Baburnama* from Chagatai language to Persian language, which was completed in 998 (1589–90) AD. He had an excellent command over the Sanskrit language.[10]

In Sanskrit, he wrote two books on astrology, Kheta-kautukam (Devanagari: खेटकौतुकम्) and Dwatrimshadyogavali (Devanagari: द्वात्रिंशद्योगावली).

Present Tomb of Abdul Rahim Khan-I-Khana[edit]

Tomb of Abdul Rahim Khan-I-Khana, Nizamuddin East, Delhi, India

His tomb is situated in Nizamuddin East on the Mathura road, near Humayun's Tomb, in New Delhi. It was built by him for his wife in 1598, and his body was placed in it in 1627.[11] In 1753-54, marble and sandstone from this tomb was used in the construction of Safdarjung's Tomb, also in New Delhi.[11][12][13][14]

In 2014, InterGlobe Foundation and the Aga Khan Trust for Culture (AKTC) announced a project to conserve and restore Abdul Rahim Khan-i-Khanan's tomb. Popularly known as Rahim and immortalised through his dohas or couplets, Rahim was among the most important ministers in Akbar's court. He was one of the Navratnas and continued to serve Salim after his accession to the throne as Emperor Jehangir. Along with taking up restoration work at the monument, AKTC also commissioned a book on Rahim titled *Abdur Rahim Khan-i-Khanan: Kavya, Saundrya & Sarthakta (Vani Prakashan).*[15] It has been edited by Harish Trivedi, with a foreword by poet-lyricist Gulzar and Urdu scholar Gopichand Narang, it has essays by academics such as Ramchandra Shukla, Namvar Singh, Uday Shankar Dubey, Sadanand Sahi, Deepa Gupta and Pratap Kumar Mishra, among others.[15]

The tomb sits prominently along the Mathura Road, formerly the Mughal Grand Trunk Road, and lies close to the Dargah of Nizamuddin Auliya and Humayun's Tomb. In 2020, after six years of restoration work by the Aga Khan Trust for Culture, Rahim Khan's tomb was opened to the public.[16] Perhaps it was the largest conservation project ever undertaken for any monument of national importance in India. For its architecture and purpose, it has often been compared with Taj Mahal.[17]

Rahim was not only a great poet but he was a great scholar and advisor, for which he became one of the navratnas of Akbar. Harka Bai, wife of Akbar-Jodha Bai, was great worshipper of Lord Krishna which influenced Rahim also. Hence, later in the life Rahim started writing Dohas on Lord Krishna. Rahim knew Farsi, Arabic and Sanskrit. He was an emotional writer but very intellectual. He wrote about detachments, policy, knowledge and general wisdom, which still makes Rahim Ke Dohe very contemporary and relevant even todays time of 2021.

Tulsidas was Rahims contemporary and was great appreciater of him. I start my book with one of the conversation between Rahim and Tulsidas.

1

Abdul Rahim was known for his strange manner of giving alms to the poor. He never looked at the person he was giving alms to, keeping his gaze downwards in all humility. When Tulsidas heard about Rahim's behaviour when giving alms, he promptly wrote a couplet and sent it to Rahim:-

Tulsidas Ask

"ऐसी देनी देंन ज्यूँ, कित सीखे हो सैन
ज्यों ज्यों कर ऊंच्यो करो, त्यों त्यों निचे नैन"

English

"Why give alms like this? Where did you learn that?
Your hands are as high as your eyes are low"

Realising that Tulsidas was well aware of the reasons behind his actions, and was merely giving him an opportunity to say a few lines in reply, he wrote to Tulsidas saying:-

Rahims Answer

"देनहार कोई और है, भेजत जो दिन रैन
लोग भरम हम पर करे, तासो निचे नैन"

English

"The Giver is someone else, giving day and night. But the world gives me the credit, so I lower my eyes."

Lessons for Entrepreneurs

Entrepreneur can learn before starting his venture is that he should not forget about the customer who is god. Any services or product which are appreciated by the customers and public in general, should be considered as blessings and the entrepreneur should always be attached to ground realities even when he is successful.

One should also remember that he should always contribute of giving back to society. Although social entrepreneurs are becoming very popular worldwide but even those who earn small profits must contribute to under-privilege. Its another way of doing karma and getting close to God.

2

रहिमन धागा प्रेम का, मत तोड़ो चटकाय।
टूटे से फिर ना मिले, मिले गाँठ परि जाय।।

रहीम दास जी कहते हैं कि प्रेम का बंधन किसी धागे के समान होता है जिसे कभी भी झटके से तोड़ नहीं देना चाहिए बल्कि उसकी हिफाजत करनी चाहिए। क्योंकि जब कोई धागा एक बार टूट जाता है तो फिर उसे जोड़ा नहीं जा सकता। जोड़ने की कोशिश में उस धागे में गाँठ पड़ जाती है। किसी से रिश्ता जब एक बार टूट जाता है तो फिर उस रिश्ते को दोबारा जोड़ा नहीं जा सकता।

English

Rahim says- It is very important to maintain good relationship with everyone. Once the trust of relationship is broken it will not remain like old relationship, as some difference will remain in mind. He compared relationship with string which once broken cannot be joined and we have to tie the knot to fix it and this knot remains throughout life.

Lesson for Entrepreneurs

Entrepreneur has to establish and maintain good trustworthy relationship with all stake holders of the business like bankers, suppliers, retailers and above all customers. One should not break their trust even if there are some setbacks and losses, and have to maintain these valuable relationship. If this trust is broken, then the business will not be same and one can permanently loose the person/partner/customer.

3

रहिमन निज मन की बिथा, मन ही राखो गोय।
सुनि अठिलैहैं लोग सब, बाँटि न लैहै कोयम।।

रहीम दास जी कहते हैं कि अपने दर्द को दूसरों से छुपा कर ही रखना चाहिए। जब आपका दर्द किसी अन्य को पता चलता है तो लोग उसका मजाक ही उड़ाते हैं। कोई भी आपके दर्द को बाँट नहीं सकता।

English

Rahim says that one should not share ones problems and sorrows with people, as the people will only laugh at you but will not share it or give any solution of your problem.

Lesson for Entrepreneurs

Entrepreneur should never discuss or disclose his organisational problem with the people whom he does not trust. People or Competitor will only enjoy your misery and will not be provide any solutions to your problems. They may also add more problems to your already existing problems and issues. Share your problem who are equally concerned with your organisation, both within and outside the organisation.

4

एकै साधे सब सधै, सब साधे सब जाय।
रहिमन मूलहिं सींचिबो, फूलै फलै अघाय।।

रहीम दास जी कहते हैं कि एक बार में कोई एक ही कार्य करना चाहिए। एक काम के पूरा होने से कई काम अपने आप हो जाते हैं। यदि एक ही साथ आप कई लक्ष्य को प्राप्त करने की कोशिश करेंगे तो कुछ भी हाथ नहीं आता। यह वैसे ही है जैसे जड़ में पानी डालने से ही किसी पौधे में फूल और फल आते हैं।

English

Rahim says that we must focus on one work at one time. If one finishes one work at one time, it automatically reflects on another work and make it easier. If you want to complete too many works at one time, none will be completed and give results. It's like giving water to the roots of the tree which then gives growth automatically to both leaves and fruits together.

Lesson for Entrepreneurs

Entrepreneur must not address too many problems of your business at one time. Instead you should take one problem and address and find solution to it. If you address too many problems at one time you will not be able to find any solution. Hence, one should learn from tree, if you water the roots, tree bear both leaves and fruits together. Hence, we should address the root cause of the problem. Many problems will be solved automatically.

5

चित्रकूट में रमि रहे, रहिमन अवध-नरेस।
जा पर बिपदा पड़त है, सो आवत यह देस।।

रहीम दास जी कहते हैं कि जब राम को बनवास मिला था तो वे चित्रकूट में रहने गये थे। चित्रकूट घनघोर वन में होने के कारण रहने लायक जगह नहीं थी। ऐसी जगह पर वही रहने जाता है जिस पर कोई भारी विपत्ति आती है।

English

Rahim says, When Lord Ram got exile from his kingdom he went to Chitrakoot for living there. However, Chitrakoot is not a place to live as it is covered with dense forest, but Ram came to live here as he was in great difficulty and need.

Lesson for Entrepreneurs

Entrepreneur should not exploit your employees as they will continue in your organisation, because they are in real need for money. Do not take advantage of their situation as they will leave as soon as they get a better option. Hence, make your organisation conducive for making your employees feel positive about the work place and this will bring very good results to the organisation also.

6

दीरघ दोहा अरथ के, आखर थोरे आहिं।
ज्यों रहीम नट कुंडली, सिमिटि कूदि चढ़ि जाहिं।।

रहीम दास जी कहते हैं कि किसी भी दोहे में कम शब्दों में ही बहुत बड़ा अर्थ छिपा होता है। यह वैसे ही होता है जैसे नट की कुंडली होती है। नट अपनी कुंडली में सिमट कर तरह तरह के विस्मयकारी करतब दिखा देता है।

English

Rahim says that we should speak less and speak when absolutely necessary and essential. Whatever we speak should be to the point and not exaggerated. It should be like snake who is hiding in small basket of snake charmer but becomes very big when out from the basket.

Lesson to Entrepreneurs

Entrepreneur has to watch what he says, as his reputation is build on that. People within the organisation and outside the organisation must trust his words. His few words must indicate his idea and vision for the organisation. Its like the snake hides in a small place but he can be really big once come out to attack his enemy.

7

धनि रहीम जल पंक को लघु जिय पियत अघाय।
उदधि बड़ाई कौन है, जगत पिआसो जाय।।

रहीम दास जी कहते हैं कि कीचड़ में पाया जाने वाला थोड़ा सा पानी ही धन्य है क्योंकि उस पानी से कितने छोटे-छोटे जीवों की प्यास बुझती है। सागर का जल विशाल मात्रा में होते हुए भी व्यर्थ होता है क्योंकि उस जल से किसी की प्यास नहीं बुझती।

English

Rahim says that even dirty water is good, as it gives small insects and species to survive. On the other hand, the great ocean water is of no use, as no one can drink that water and survive for life. Hence, dirty water is better than ocean water.

Lesson to Entrepreneurs

Entrepreneurs should remember that helping people in need is more crucial than when they actually need it. It's immaterial when you have money but it's of no use to people around you. They can be your employees, they can be your friends and they can be your relatives. Always help them when they require and not when you think its comfortable for you. Your money will be like ocean water; you have plenty but no one need it.

8

नाद रीझि तन देत मृग, नर धन देत समेत।
ते रहीम पशु से अधिक, रीझेहु कछू न देत।।

रहीम दास जी कहते हैं कि हिरण किसी के संगीत से खुश होकर अपना शरीर न्योछावर कर देता है। इसी तरह से कुछ लोग दूसरे के प्रेम से खुश होकर अपना सब कुछ दे देते हैं। लेकिन कुछ लोग पशु से भी बदतर होते हैं जो दूसरों से तो बहुत कुछ ले लेते हैं लेकिन बदले में कुछ भी नहीं देते हैं।

English

Rahim says, When a Deer is mesmerized with music and falls in love with it, he can surrender completely to the person. Similarly, a person who falls in love with someone give in totality. Rahim continues that if the person do love someone but only takes from them and gives back nothing, he is worse than a animal.

Lesson for Entrepreneurs

Entrepreneur when love something like his country, organisation or people you have to give back something to them in return. Maybe thru Social Responsibility, HR practices and building relationship with your employees. If you donot do it will not last long and will end in disasterours results.

9

बिगरी बात बनै नहीं, लाख करौ किन कोय।
रहिमन फाटे दूध को, मथे न माखन होय।।

रहीम दास जी कहते हैं कि कोई बात जब एक बार बिगड़ जाती है तो लाख कोशिश के बावजूद उसे ठीक नहीं किया जा सकता। यह वैसे ही है जैसे जब दूध एक बार फट जाये तो फिर उसको मथने से मक्खन नहीं निकलता।

English

Rahim says that it is very important to understand relationship because if its go wrong then it is very difficult to make it work. It's like milk once spoiled it cannot be used again even after great effort. Hence, we should also take same care of our relationship very seriously.

Lesson for Entrepreneurs

Entrepreneur should understand that it's important that relationship building with all stake holders is very important and delicate. Every stake holder like customers, employees, bankers, suppliers etc has different kind of relationship, which has to be kept sacred at all cost. If it is broken, then it is very difficult to rebuild it.

10

रहिमन देखि बड़ेन को, लघु न दीजिये डारि।
जहाँ काम आवे सुई, कहा करे तरवारि।।

रहीम दास जी कहते हैं कि किसी बड़ी चीज को देखकर किसी छोटी चीज की उपेक्षा नहीं करनी चाहिए। क्योंकि जहाँ छोटी चीज की जरूरत होती है वहाँ पर बड़ी चीज बेकार हो जाती है। जैसे जहाँ सुई की जरूरत होती है वहाँ तलवार का कोई काम नहीं होता।

English

Rahim says that it is important not to ignore the small persons, as they are also useful in their own work. When you want a needle to stitch some cloth, it cannot be done by the big sword.

Lesson for Entrepreneurs

When Entrepreneur become successful businessman or your organisation becomes big, never forget the junior employees who stood by you, during your earlier and difficult times. Also what juniors can do it cannot be done by senior employees. Hence, one should always take care of junior employees also like senior ones.

11

रहिमन निज संपत्ति बिन, कौ न बिपति सहाय।
बिनु पानी ज्यों जलज को, नहिं रवि सके बचाय।।

रहीम दास जी कहते हैं कि जब आपके पास धन नहीं होता है तो कोई भी विपत्ति में आपकी सहायता नहीं करता। यह वैसे ही है जैसे यदि तालाब सूख जाता है तो कमल को सूर्य जैसा प्रतापी भी नहीं बचा पाता है।

English

Rahim says that when the person who does not have money, nobody comes forward and help him, when he is in distress or problem. It's like same when pond water is dry not even Lotus flower can bloom in it, which needs not much water.

Lesson for Entrepreneurs

Entrepreneur should be very careful when we are dealing with finance. When there is no money with entrepreneur, no one comes forward to help you. Every one will make excuses. Hence, it is very important to manage properly our finance and spend on things which are extremely necessary for the venture/business.

12

रहिमन पानी राखिए, बिनु पानी सब सून।
पानी गए न ऊबरै, मोती, मानुज़, चून।।

रहीम दास जी कहते हैं कि पानी हमेशा अपने पास रखना चाहिए क्योंकि पानी के बगैर जीवन असंभव है। बिना पानी के न तो मोती बनता है, न चूना और पानी के बिना मनुष्य जीवन भी असंभव है।

English

Rahim says here that water is very precious for life, without water life cannot exist. He further says that without water there will be no pearl in sea and no Choona which is used for eating. Similarly, without water human life will be non-existence.

Lesson for Entrepreneurs

Entrepreneur must know that no business can exist without human beings. Without good human resource your business cannot survive. Hence, we should take all possible care of our employees and their problems. Without good human resource we cannot continue our business for long.

13

छिमा बड़न को चाहिये, छोटन को उतपात।
कह रहीम हरि का घट्यौ, जो भृगु मारी लात।।

रहीम दास जी कहते हैं कि बड़ों को क्षमा शोभा देती है और छोटों को उत्पात (बदमाशी)। अर्थात अगर छोटे बदमाशी करें कोई बड़ी बात नहीं और बड़ों को इस बात पर क्षमा कर देना चाहिए। छोटे अगर उत्पात मचाएं तो उनका उत्पात भी छोटा ही होता है। जैसे यदि कोई कीड़ा (भृगु) अगर लात मारे भी तो उससे कोई हानि नहीं होती।

English

Rahim here says that it is important for elders to ignore the mistakes of younger people, as their mistakes are also very small. It's like mosquitoes biting you and you donot have to bite it back. Rahim says that elders should ignore and pardon small mistakes of younger people.

Lesson for Entrepreneurs

Rahim says here that if some employees do small mistakes, the seniors must guide them and ignore the mistakes. When new people start working they do small mistakes which could be excused, but they must be guided also not to repeat it.

14

तरुवर फल नहिं खात है, सरवर पियहि न पान।
कहि रहीम पर काज हित, संपति सँचहि सुजान।।

रहीम दास जी कहते हैं कि वृक्ष अपने फल स्वयं नहीं खाते हैं और सरोवर भी अपना पानी स्वयं नहीं पीता है। इसी तरह अच्छे और सज्जन व्यक्ति वो हैं जो दूसरों के कार्य के लिए संपत्ति को संचित करते हैं।

English

Rahim says like tree does not eat its own fruits and sea does not drink its own water, similarly good and learned people are those, who use their wisdom and knowledge for the society and not themselves.

Lesson for Entrepreneurs

Entrepreneurs must realise that whatever is the profit of the organisation, it should give back to organisational growth and must not keep anything for oneself. It can be used for your own employees or can be used outside the organisation for welfare of the society at large.

15

दुख में सुमिरन सब करे, सुख में करे न कोय।
जो सुख में सुमिरन करे, तो दुख काहे होय।।

इस दोहे में संत रहीम दास जी कहते हैं कि दुख में सभी लोग याद करते हैं, सुख में कोई नहीं। यदि सुख में भी याद करते तो दुख होता ही नहीं।

English

Rahim says that people always remember god/almighty in the time of distress and sorrow, but never remember God when they are prosperous and happy. So if people remember God in good times, why bad times will come.

Lesson for Entrepreneurs

When the organisation is earning huge profits, owners forget about their employees. But once there are losses and problems, you start remembering your employees. So if you share your happiness when the times are good with your employees, then why bad times will come to your organisation. Hence, always take good care of your employees all time and bad times will never come.

16

खैर, खून, खाँसी, खुसी, बैर, प्रीति, मदपान।
रहिमन दाबे न दबै, जानत सकल जहान।।

इस दोहे में संत रहीम दास जी कहते हैं कि दुनिया जानती है कि खैरियत, खून, खांसी, खुशी, दुश्मनी, प्रेम और मदिरा का नशा छुपाए नहीं छुपता है।

English

Rahim says that feelings of good wishes, blood, cough, happiness, enemity, love and intoxication cannot be hidden despite all efforts.

Lesson for Entrepreneurs

It is important that entrepreneur should express their views freely and also allow their employees to express their views and feelings. They should speak without fear and put their views in front of the seniors. This will help the organisation immensely.

17

जो रहीम ओछो बढ़ै, तौ अति ही इतराय।
प्यादे सों फरजी भयो, टेढ़ो टेढ़ो जाय।।

रहीम दास जी कहते हैं कि ओछे लोग जब प्रगति करते हैं तो बहुत ही इतराते हैं। वैसे ही जैसे शतरंज के खेल में जब प्यादा फरजी बन जाता है तो वह टेढ़ी चाल चलने लगता है।

English

Rahim says that when people with small mentality gets success they start to show off their wealth a lot. It's like in the game of Chess when Soldier becomes Farzi they start walking diagonally.

Lesson for Entrepreneurs

It indicates that if Entrepreneur become successful, he must remain grounded otherwise it will be disasterous for your business and self. Always take your success with mental balance and maturity. Success is temporary and will come and go, hence, one should be always remain focused.

18

रहिमन थोरे दिनन को, कौन करे मुहँ स्याह
नहीं छलन को परतिया, नहीं कारन को ब्याह

रहीम दास जी कहते हैं कि थोड़े दिन के लिए कौन अपना मुंह काला करता हैं क्यूंकि पर नारी को ना धोखा दिया जा सकता हैं और ना ही विवाह किया जा सकता है।

English

Rahim says that why one should look for other women as neither you can run away from that lady nor you can marry her.

Lesson for Entrepreneurs

Entrepreneur should not depend on some other person's wealth, as you can neither leave it nor that will be your own. Hence, we should focus on only our wealth and what is our, and that is the true ownership of the asset.

19

आब गई आदर गया, नैनन गया सनेहि।
ये तीनों तब ही गये, जबहि कहा कछु देहि।।

इस दोहे में रहीम दास जी कहते हैं कि ज्यों ही कोई किसी से कुछ मांगता है त्यों ही आबरू, आदर और आंख से प्रेम चला जाता है।

English

Rahim says that the moment you ask for money from some one, you loose three things- Dignity, Respect and Love. Hence, we must always avoid asking for money from anyone and not to loose three important things of our lives.

Lesson for Entrepreneurs

Entrepreneur when in business, should not ask for financial help from anyone. You will loose all respect, love and dignity from that person. It is better to arrange your own funds thru other methods like banks and investors purely on professional basis.

20

खीरा सिर ते काटिये, मलियत नमक लगाय।
रहिमन करुये मुखन को, चहियत इहै सजाय।।

रहीम दास जी कहते हैं कि खीरे को सिर से काटना चाहिए और उस पर नमक लगाना चाहिए। यदि किसी के मुंह से कटु वाणी निकले तो उसे भी यही सजा होनी चाहिए।

English

Rahim says that like when cucumber is sour you put salt on the top of cucumber and take out the sourness of the cucumber. Similarly, if any one speaks bad with you the same treatment should be given to that person.

Lesson for Entrepreneurs

As an entrepreneur you should take rapid action against those who speak wrong and without basis against your business. They should be shown no mercy as to how they should be treated. They should be treated ruthlessly and without mercy, to give an example to others.

21

चाह गई चिंता मिटी, मनुआ बेपरवाह।
जिनको कछु नहि चाहिये, वे साहन के साह।।

रहीम दास जी कहते हैं कि जिन्हें कुछ नहीं चाहिए वो राजाओं के राजा हैं। क्योंकि उन्हें ना तो किसी चीज की चाह है, ना ही चिंता और मन तो बिल्कुल बेपरवाह है।

English

Rahim says that if you are not worried about anything in your life, you will be King of Kings. If you donot desire anything, you will be less worried and your mental level will always be at peace.

Lesson for Entrepreneurs

If Entrepreneur have no ambition for himself personally, then the business will do extremely well. One should always think of business growth rather than your own personal growth. If you do that it will bring the best results for the business and bring prosperity to all, including you also.

22

जे गरीब पर हित करैं, हे रहीम बड़ लोग।
कहा सुदामा बापुरो, कृष्ण मिताई जोग।।

इस दोहे में रहीम दास जी कहते हैं कि जो गरीब का हित करते हैं वो बड़े लोग होते हैं। जैसे सुदामा कहते हैं कृष्ण की दोस्ती भी एक साधना है।

English

Rahim says that those who help poor people are big persons. It's like when Sudama have friendship with Lord Krishna it is also like worship. Hence, helping poor people is also like worshipping god.

Lesson for Entrepreneurs

It implies that even when business is doing great, one should not forget about the people who need help from prosperous and rich people. We should always help them as much as we can, and take it as part of social responsibility. It will bring more success to business and great satisfaction to oneself.

23

जो रहीम गति दीप की, कुल कपूत गति सोय।
बारे उजियारो लगे, बढ़े अँधेरो होय।।

संत रहीम जी कहते हैं कि दीपक के चरित्र जैसा ही कुपुत्र का भी चरित्र होता है। दोनों ही पहले तो उजाला करते हैं पर बढ़ने के साथ-साथ अंधेरा होता जाता है।

English

Rahim says here that the qualities of lamp and bad son is same. Initially both give joy, light and happiness but later they create darkness in the life.

Lesson for Entrepreneurs

It is very important to rightly guide your chidren from childhood and groom them to be good human being and businessmen. Otherwise they will bring end to your flourishing business and bring darkness to you.

24

रहिमन देख बड़ेन को, लघु न दीजिये डारि।
जहाँ काम आवै सुई, कहा करै तलवारि।।

इस दोहे में संत रहीम जी कहते हैं कि बड़ों को देखकर छोटों को भगा नहीं देना चाहिए। क्योंकि जहां छोटे का काम होता है वहां बड़ा कुछ नहीं कर सकता। जैसे कि सुई के काम को तलवार नहीं कर सकती।

English

Rahim says that when you become successful and big person donot forget the workers, as where you need needle you cannot use a sword. Hence, everyone is important in each job.

Lesson for Entrepreneurs

It implies that when you and your organisation become big, you should not forget people who helped you in your success. Always remember them and help them whatever you are able to do so.

25

बड़े काम ओछो करै, तो न बड़ाई होय।
ज्यों रहीम हनुमंत को, गिरिधर कहे न कोय।।

संत रहीम जी कहते हैं कि जब ओछे लक्ष्य के लिए लोग बड़े काम करते हैं तो उनकी बड़ाई नहीं होती है। जब हनुमान जी ने पर्वत को उठाया था तो उनका नाम 'गिरिधर' नहीं पड़ा क्योंकि उन्होंने पर्वत राज को क्षति पहुंचाई थी, पर जब श्री कृष्ण ने पर्वत उठाया तो उनका नाम 'गिरिधर' पड़ा क्योंकि उन्होंने सर्व जन की रक्षा हेतु पर्वत को उठाया था।

English

Rahim says that when you work for selfish and small motives you are not respected and recognized. Like when Hanumanji lifted Mountain it was for one person and small motive and hence, he was not called Giridhar. However, when Lord Krishna lifted Govardhan mountain for the safety of the people at large, he was called Giridhar. Hence, Motive and Intention is very important.

Lesson for Entrepreneurs

It implies that when your business motive is good and successful it is always applauded. On the other hand, when your business is very successful but it is not ethical and fair and self centered, you donot get respect and dignity from the people and society.

26

माली आवत देख के, कलियन करे पुकारि।
फूले फूले चुनि लिये, कालि हमारी बारि।।

इस दोहे में संत रहीम जी कहते हैं कि माली को आते देखकर कलियां कहती हैं कि आज तो उसने फूल चुन लिया पर कल को हमारी बारी भी आएगी क्योंकि कल हम भी खिलकर फूल हो जाएंगे।

English

Rahim says when a gardner goes to garden, buds say to each other, that today gardner is picking flowers but tomorrow he will come back and pick us, as we will become flower from buds.

Lesson for Entrepreneurs

It implies that when we see problem of others, we should not ignore it. As one day the same problem will come on our business also. Hence, it is important to realise the problem and find a solution to it.

27

एकहि साधै सब सधै, सब साधे सब जाय।
रहिमन मूलहि सींचबो, फूलहि फलहि अघाय।।

संत रहीम जी कहते हैं कि एक को साधने से सब साधते हैं। सब को साधने से सभी के जाने की आशंका रहती है। वैसे ही जैसे किसी पौधे के जड़ मात्र को सींचने से फूल और फल सभी को पानी प्राप्त हो जाता है और उन्हें अलग-अलग सींचने की जरूरत नहीं होती है। इसलिए केवल परमात्मा में ही ध्यान लगाना चाहिए।

English

Rahim says that it is better that we focus on the main issues and not those issues which are not so important or relevant. It's like when we water the roots of a tree, fruits and leaves are automatically taken care of.

Lesson for Entrepreneurs

It implies that if we focus on the main problems of the business, we automatically address the non-important issues. Hence, we must focus on real problem of the organisation which will automatically solve the other minor or smaller issues.

28

रहिमन वे नर मर गये, जे कछु माँगन जाहि।
उनते पहिले वे मुये, जिन मुख निकसत नाहि।।

संत रहीम जी कहते हैं कि जो व्यक्ति किसी से कुछ मांगने के लिए जाता है वो तो मरे हुए हैं ही परन्तु उससे पहले ही वे लोग मर जाते हैं जिनके मुंह से कुछ भी नहीं निकलता है।

English

Rahim says that when anyone goes asking for help or support, he is worse than dead. But worser are those who can help but they refuse to help others.

Lesson for the Entrepreneurs

It implies that when you are going to someone asking for help you are worse than dead. Hence, we should not go asking for help for the organisation, one should grow with its own means and capabilities. On the other hand, if we are in a position to help other, but we refuse then it is worse than anything else.

29

रहिमन विपदा ही भली, जो थोरे दिन होय।
हित अनहित या जगत में, जानि परत सब कोय।।

संत रहीम जी कहते हैं कि कुछ दिन रहने वाली विपदा अच्छी होती है। क्योंकि इसी दौरान यह पता चलता है कि दुनिया में कौन हमारा हित या अहित सोचता है।

English

Rahim says that when the problem is for some time it is good. Because during this time person comes to know who will stand by him during bad times, and who will disappear when you need them.

Lesson for Entrepreneurs

It implies that it is sometime better that your organisation undergoes some challenges/ problems. These challenges will prove who stands by the organisation and who will not stand by you, when your organisation is in trouble.

30

बड़ा हुआ तो क्या हुआ, जैसे पेड़ खजूर।
पंथी को छाया नहीं, फल लागे अति दूर।।

संत रहीम जी कहते हैं कि बड़े होने का यह मतलब नहीं है कि उससे किसी का भला न हो। जैसे खजूर का पेड़ तो बहुत बड़ा होता है परन्तु उसका फल इतना दूर होता है कि तोड़ना मुश्किल का काम है।

English

Rahim says it is immaterial that you are big and you are of no use to others. You are like Khajoor Tree which is very long but it has no shades and no one can enjoy the fruits (dates) as it is beyond the reach of common man.

Lesson for Entrepreneurs

It implies that if your business is successful and you are not helping the people or society at large, the success is of no use. One should always contribute to the wellness of the society and give back to your people, who has made the organisation successful and grow.

31

रहिमन चुप हो बैठिये, देखि दिनन के फेर।
जब नीके दिन आइहैं, बनत न लगिहैं देर।।

संत रहीम जी कहते हैं कि जब बुरे दिन आए हों तो चुप ही बैठना चाहिए, क्योंकि जब अच्छे दिन आते हैं तब बात बनते देर नहीं लगती।

English

Rahim says that when time is not good, one should have patience and wait for time to pass. When that bad phase is gone everything will work accordingly and automatically.

Lesson for the Entrepreneurs

It implies that when your organisation is undergoing trouble then you should have patience and let the things passby. You should do the best in that times and wait for the results. One should not get worried about the problems as when the time is fine, things will become good automatically and company will be out of trouble and everything will be fine with the organisation.

32

बानी ऐसी बोलिये, मन का आपा खोय।
औरन को सीतल करै, आपहु सीतल होय।।

संत रहीम जी कहते हैं कि अपने मन से अहंकार को निकालकर ऐसी बात करनी चाहिए जिसे सुनकर दूसरों को खुशी हो और खुद भी खुश हों।

English

Rahim says it is important not to have arrogance in oneself but we should speak in such a way that makes people happy. Good speech bring joy not only to listners but also to the person who speaks it.

Lesson for Entrepreneurs

It implies that communication is very important in doing business. It is important how to say things and without hurting anyone. It will make the problem vanish if we have cordial relationship through good communication.

33

मन मोती अरु दूध रस, इनकी सहज सुभाय।
फट जाये तो ना मिले, कोटिन करो उपाय।।

इस दोहे में रहीम जी कहते हैं कि मन, मोती, फूल, दूध और रस जब तक सहज और सामान्य रहते हैं तो अच्छे लगते हैं परन्तु यदि एक बार वे फट जाएं तो करोड़ों उपाय कर लो वे फिर वापस अपने सहज रूप में नहीं आते।

English

Rahim says that when Mind, Pearl, Flower, Milk and Juice remains in normal condition it is good. But if they are spoiled then nothing can be done to bring it to normal condition.

Lesson for Entrepreneurs

It implies that one should always keep the mind in a balanced condition. Only then you can tackle the problem and solve them. If your mind is not stable you will never be able to tackle issues of your organisation and solve them. Hence, balanced mind is important for entrepreneurs.

34

रहिमन ओछे नरन सो, बैर भली ना प्रीत।
काटे चाटे स्वान के, दोउ भाँति विपरीत।।

संत रहीम जी कहते हैं कि कम दिमाग के व्यक्तियों से ना तो प्रीती और ना ही दुश्मनी अच्छी होती है। जैसे कुत्ता चाहे काटे या चाटे दोनों को विपरीत नहीं माना जाता है।

English

Rahim says that it is important to keep distance from bad people, as neither their closeness nor their enemity is good. It is like relation with dog, neither their saliva is good nor their bite is good for human being, both are dangerous for the health of the person.

Lesson for Entrepreneurs

It implies that as an entrepreneur, you should always take the path of clean business. One should not be lured by illegal ways of profit making. One should always avoid people who recommend such things to you and one must keep distance from them.

35

रहिमन उजली प्रकृति को नहीं नीच को संग
करिया वासन कर गहे कालिख लागत अंग।

संत रहीम जी कहते हैं कि अच्छे लोगों को नीच लोगों की संगति नहीं करनी चाहिये। कालिख लगे बरतन को पकड़ने से हाथ काले हो जाते हैं। नीच लोगों के साथ बदनामी का दाग लग जाता है।

English

Rahim says that it is important for good people to avoid company of bad people. It is like that if you lift a black utensil, your hands will certainly get dirty. Hence, if good person will accompany bad people certainly they will be also infamous. Hence, avoid those people.

Lesson for Entrepreneurs

It implies that it is important with whom one should business. Even if its advantageous and profitable to do business with wrong people, one should always avoid it. As one day they will create some big problem for you. Hence, have business with good people even if the profits are low.

36

समय पाय फल होत है, समय पाय झरी जात।
सदा रहे नहिं एक सी, का रहीम पछितात।।

रहीम दास कहते हैं कि उपयुक्त समय आने पर वृक्ष में फल लगता है। झड़ने का समय आने पर वह झड़ जाता है। सदा किसी की अवस्था एक जैसी नहीं रहती, इसलिए दुःख के समय पछताना व्यर्थ है।

English

Rahim says it is important to wait for the right time to have fruit from tree. If you delay and come in time of fall season, then no fruits will be available. Similarly, we should not lament when we face sorrow as that condition will never remain the same for very long and will change for good later.

Lesson for Entrepreneurs

It implies that we should face our problem without any worries, as the time will pass also and one will get out of trouble. We should tackle our business problem with balanced mind and keeping faith that this challenging time will also get over soon.

37

वे रहीम नर धन्य हैं, पर उपकारी अंग।
बांटन वारे को लगे, ज्यों मेंहदी को रंग।।

रहीम कहते हैं कि वे लोग धन्य हैं जिनका शरीर सदा सबका उपकार करता है। जिस प्रकार मेंहदी बांटने वाले के अंग पर भी मेंहदी का रंग लग जाता है, उसी प्रकार परोपकारी का शरीर भी सुशोभित रहता है।

English

Rahim says that those are great people who are always doing some good work and helping the needy. It is like Heena which although bring colour and fragrance which it brings to other person, but it is self giving good fragrance on itself.

Lesson for Entrepreneurs

It implies that we should always help the people who are needy and looking for help. It not only brings joy to whom you help but also gives immense pleasure to one self also. Hence, we should always look for opportunity for helping others in society and bring joy to all involved.

38

पावस देखि रहीम मन, कोइल साधे मौन।
अब दादुर वक्ता भए, हमको पूछे कौन।।

रहीम कहते हैं कि वे लोग धन्य हैं वर्षा ऋतु को देखकर कोयल और रहीम के मन ने मौन साध लिया है। अब तो मेंढक ही बोलने वाले हैं। हमारी तो कोई बात ही नहीं पूछता। अभिप्राय यह है कि कुछ अवसर ऐसे आते हैं जब गुणवान को चुप रह जाना पड़ता है। उनका कोई आदर नहीं करता और गुणहीन वाचाल व्यक्तियों का ही बोलबाला हो जाता है।

English

Rahim says that when it is rainy season Koyal (bird) remains silent, as they know now only Frogs will make noises. Similary some time it is important for wise people to remain silent and let other speaks, because even if you speak no one will listen to you. Only the notorious people will be listened at that time. Hence, it is better to remain silent.

Lesson for Entrepreneurs

It implies that when it's not good time for the organisation, one should not start explaining the causes of the problems. As at that time only critics will criticize you and people will listen to them only. Hence, it is better to remain silent and wait for your turn to speak in good times.

39

रहिमन अंसुवा नयन ढरि, जिय दुःख प्रगट करेइ,
जाहि निकारौ गेह ते, कस न भेद कहि देइ

रहीम कहते हैं की आंसू नयनों से बहकर मन का दुःख प्रकट कर देते हैं। सत्य ही है कि जिसे घर से निकाला जाएगा वह घर का भेद दूसरों से कह ही देगा।

English

Rahim says that when tears leave your eyes it shows that you are having sorrow. Similarly, when truth or reality leaves the house then it will tell everyone about the inside stories of the house.

Lesson for the Entrepreneurs

It implies that it is important that your people donot leave your organisation and tell the secrets to your competitors. Hence, we should always keep the important and good people in organisation, as they are priceless and important for organisational survival.

40

दोनों रहिमन एक से, जों लों बोलत नाहिं
जान परत हैं काक पिक, रितु बसंत के माहिं

रहीम कहते हैं की कौआ और कोयल रंग में एक समान होते हैं। जब तक ये बोलते नहीं तब तक इनकी पहचान नहीं हो पाती। लेकिन जब वसंत ऋतु आती है तो कोयल की मधुर आवाज से दोनों का अंतर स्पष्ट हो जाता है।

English

Rahim says that Crow and Koyal (bird) both have same colour, one cannot distinguish till they speak. But when rainy season comes and they speak then you come to know the difference between the two.

Lesson for Entrepreneurs

It is important that when we speak we should be speaking sensibily and able to communicate well with the others. We should not speak without sense and without meaning.

41

जैसी परे सो सहि रहे, कहि रहीम यह देह.
धरती ही पर परत है, सीत घाम औ मेह

रहीम जी कहते हैं कि जैसी इस देह पर पड़ती है– सहन करनी चाहिए, क्योंकि इस धरती पर ही सर्दी, गर्मी और वर्षा पड़ती है। अर्थात जैसे धरती शीत, धूप और वर्षा सहन करती है, उसी प्रकार शरीर को सुख-दुःख सहन करना चाहिए।

English

Rahim says that mother earth tolerates seasons and its difficulties of summer, cold and rain. Similarly, we should also tolerate happiness and sorrows of life and continue with it in a positive way.

Lesson for Entrepreneurs

It implies that organisation will go through many challenges and problems/ losses and profits etc. However, one should look it as a passing phase and continue its work in a positive manner. Hence, we should take ups and downs of business as part of business cycle and continue it with positive mind.

42

जो बड़ेन को लघु कहें, नहीं रहीम घटी जाहिं
गिरधर मुरलीधर कहें, कछु दुःख मानत नाहिं

रहीम कहते हैं कि बड़े को छोटा कहने से बड़े का बड़प्पन नहीं घटता, क्योंकि गिरिधर (कृष्ण) को मुरलीधर कहने से उनकी महिमा में कमी नहीं होती।

English

Rahim says if some one calls you unimportant and small, it should not effect you. It's like calling Lord Krishna Murlidhar (Flute Owner) which Lord Krishan also enjoyed the name and was popular. It does not make Lord Krishna anything less.

Lesson for Entrepreneurs

It implies that if some one belittle you, one should not be worried or get hurt. Actually it does not make you small. One should know its worth and let people say anything about you or about your organisation. It should not effect working of your organisation and yourself.

43

रूठे सुजन मनाइए, जो रूठे सौ बार
रहिमन फिरि-फिरि पोइए, टूटे मुक्ता हार

रहीम कहते हैं कि यदि आपका प्रिय सौ बार भी रूठे, तो भी रूठे हुए प्रिय को मनाना चाहिए, क्योंकि यदि मोतियों की माला टूट जाए तो उन मोतियों को बार-बार धागें में पिरो लेना चाहिए।

English

Rahim says that when anyone near and dear to you is upset, you should always go and talk to them and clear doubts.Even if you have to do that 100 times, you must do it. It's like if neckless of pearls is broken 100 times, you still weave it back and bring all pearls together.

Lesson for Entrepreneurs

It implies that when you see someone upset in your organisation, you should go and talk to them umpteen times. As they are priceless and they are important for your organisation and yourself.

44

जो रहीम उत्तम प्रकृति, का करी सकत कुसंग।
चन्दन विष व्यापे नहीं, लिपटे रहत भुजंग।।

रहीम कहते हैं कि जो अच्छे स्वभाव के मनुष्य होते हैं, उनको बुरी संगति भी बिगाड़ नहीं पाती। जहरीले सांप चन्दन के वृक्ष से लिपटे रहने पर भी उस पर कोई जहरीला प्रभाव नहीं डाल पाते।

English

Rahim says that people who are good, remains good even in company of bad people. It's like there are snake on the sandal tree with deadly vemon, but still sandal tree does not leave its good aroma and fragrance.

Lesson for Entrepreneurs

It implies that it is immaterial with whom you should be doing business with, but it is important that you are truthful and clean doing business with them. You will never be effected by their dubious way of doing business and will not be in any trouble as your business practices are clean.

45

रहिमन मनहि लगाई कै, देखि लेहू किन कोय।
नर को बस करिबो कहा, नारायन बस होय।।

रहीम जी कहते हैं कि शत प्रतिशत मन लगाकर किये गए काम को देखें, उसमें कैसी सफलता मिलती है। अगर अच्छी नियत और मेहनत से कोई भी काम किया जाए तो सफलता मिलती ही है क्योंकि सही एवं उचित परिश्रम से इंसान ही नहीं भगवान को भी जीता जा सकता है।

English

Rahim says that whatever work we take we should do it with great zeal and truthfulness. With truthness and pure heart you can not only win people but also the God.

Lesson for Entrepreneurs

It implies that if we do our work with pure heart and truthfulness, success will certainly come to our doorsteps. With such good intention you can achieve anything which you set your target on.

46

यह रहीम निज संग लै, जनमत जगत न कोय
बैर, प्रीति, अभ्यास जस, होत होत ही होय

रहीम जी कहते हैं कि दुश्मनी, प्रेम, अभ्यास और यश या मान-सम्मान कोई मनुष्य अपने साथ लेकर पैदा नहीं होता। यह चीजें धीरे-धीरे मनुष्य के आचरण और प्रयासों के साथ बढ़ती हैं।

English

Rahim says that no one is born with enemity, love, practice, popularity. It slowly comes to the person with his conduct and efforts only.

Lesson for Entrepreneurs

It implies that as an entrepreneur you can have enemies, friends, popularity, respect etc according to your conduct and of the organisation. Hence, one should always focus on the good things and ignore which are bad for the organisation.

47

रहिमन वहां न जाइये, जहाँ कपट को हेत।
हम तो ढारत ढेकुली, सींचत अपनों खेत।।

रहीमदास जी कहते हैं कि वहां नहीं जाना चाहिए जहाँ छल कपट का बोलबाला हो तथा लोग छल कपट से अपना कार्य पूरा करते हों। क्योंकि हम तो मेहनत करके कुँए से पानी खींचते हैं और छल कपट करने वाले लोग बिना मेहनत के ही अपना खेत सींच लेते हैं।

English

Rahim says that one should not go where there are people involved in illegal things and adopt unethical practices. As you will with great effort take out the water from the well but these people will grab it and use your water for their own farm.

Lesson for Entrepreneurs

It implies that despite great incentives and lucrative offers we should not be lured by any unethical person or practices. Ultimately those people will be benefitted by our efforts and take the profits and we will be always at loss. Hence, avoid them.

48

बड़े बड़ाई ना करैं, बड़ो न बोले बोल।
रहिमन हीरा कब कहे, लाख टका है मोल।

रहीमदास जी कहते हैं कि जो लोग वास्तव में बड़े होते हैं वो बड़ी-बड़ी बातें नहीं करते हैं तथा कभी भी अपनी बड़ाई अपने मुंह से नहीं करते हैं। हीरा अपने आप कभी नहीं कहता है कि मेरी कीमत लाख रूपये है।

English

Rahim says that great people never boast about their own greatness. It's like Diamond never tell its own price. It's others who tell how great the person is or how valuable the Diamond is.

Lesson for Entrepreneurs

It implies that when your organisation become big never boast about its greatness. It is very important that people must say that and realise how great is your organisation.

49

सब को सब कोऊ करै कै सलाम कै राम
हित 'रहीम' तब जानिए जब कछु अटकै काम

रहीमदास जी कहते हैं कि लोग राम-राम या सलाम तो सब को करते हैं पर जो मुश्किल परिस्थिति में काम आये वही अपना होता है।

English

Rahim says that many people will meet and greet you when you are doing good and will be your well wishers. But the real well wisher is that person who helps you in the time of need.

Lessons for Entrepreneurs

When you are successful in your life there will be many friends and well wishers and would like to have association with you. But the real well wisher is that who stand by you, help you in the time of need.

50

तासों ही कछु पाइए, कीजे जाकी आस
रीते सरवर पर गए, कैसे बुझे पियास

रहीमदास जी कहते हैं कि आशा भी उसी से की जानी चाहिए जिससे कुछ प्राप्त होने की संभावना हो क्योंकि खाली सरोवर किसी की प्यास नहीं बुझा सकता।

English

Rahim says that when you are in need you should go to only those people who can actually help you. Going to other person will be futile. It's like when you are thirsty you go to a pond which has water, and not to that well which has no water and cannot quench your thirst.

Lessons for Entrepreneurs

It implies that when your organisation is going through a rough passage you should look for help from only those people who can actually help you out from that situation. Never go to person and tell your problem, who cannot help you.